For

FRIENDS ARE
AS GOOD AS
Gold

WRITTEN AND COMPILED BY
SARAH M. HUPP

DESIGNED BY
KERREN BARBAS

PETER PAUPER PRESS, INC.
WHITE PLAINS, NEW YORK

*For my family,
because of your
encouragement,
patience and love*

Text copyright © 2000
Peter Pauper Press, Inc.
202 Mamaroneck Avenue
White Plains, NY 10601
All rights reserved
ISBN 0-88088-109-7
Printed in China
7 6 5 4 3 2 1

*I*ntroduction

The legend of King Midas
recounts the folly
of the pursuit of wealth
to the exclusion of all else.

Midas failed to learn
that the world's greatest treasure
is to be found in the
companionship of friends.

When one
is surrounded by friends,
one is truly rich, for
Friends Are as Good as Gold.

S. M. H.

*M*inds touch
Hearts overlap
Souls bond
Life is enriched
A friendship is forged.

*F*riendship is invaluable;
it cannot be bought, begged,
borrowed or stolen.
Yes, friendship
has no value to anyone
unless it is given freely.

*F*riendship is a living thing
that lasts only as long as it is
nourished with kindness,
sympathy, and understanding.
E. C. McKenzie

*F*riendship is one of the most
tangible things in a world which
offers fewer and fewer supports.
Kenneth Branagh

*G*ood friends who are kind and
loving act like a magnet, drawing
these self-same characteristics
from deep within us.

We were trying
to put up a fence before
a storm hit, but we lacked
the proper tools needed to
stretch the fencing into place.

A kindly stranger saw
our problem, stopped, and pulled
just the tool we needed
from the back of his truck.

Gratefully shaking his hand, we
asked the man what kind of work
he did for a living.
He merely smiled and said,
"I work at making friends."

*F*riendship consists
in forgetting what one gives, and
remembering what one receives.
ALEXANDRE DUMAS,
THE ELDER

*G*reat souls by instinct
to each other turn,
Demand alliance,
and in friendship burn.
JOSEPH ADDISON

*P*ain caused by a close friend
can be forgiven because it is
accompanied by love.

*F*riend:
one who knows
all about you and loves you just
the same.
ELBERT HUBBARD

*F*riendship is the common
path that leads us into life's very
heart.
EUGENE KENNEDY

*T*he world is round
so that friendship may encircle it.
E. C. MCKENZIE

*W*hen you have found
someone you can talk to
endlessly but who doesn't need
words to know how you feel,
you have found a friend.

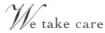

*W*e take care
of our health, we lay up money,
we make our roof tight
and our clothing sufficient,
but who provides wisely
that he shall not be wanting
in the best property of
all — friends?

RALPH WALDO EMERSON

*B*lessed thing it is
for any man or woman to have
a friend; one human soul
whom we can trust utterly;
who knows the best and the
worst of us, and who loves us,
in spite of our faults: who will
speak the honest truth to us,
while the world flatters us
to our faces . . . , but who,
again will comfort and
encourage us in the day
of difficulty and sorrow,
when the world leaves us alone
to fight our own battles
as we can.

CHARLES KINGSLEY

*F*riendship involves
a concern for and involvement
with the well-being
of another.
DAVID W. SMITH

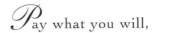

*P*ay what you will,
but you cannot purchase
friendship. If one avows fealty
after the receipt of a gift,
that is not friendship
but rather a safeguard to ensure
future bounty to oneself.

A gardener may view a friend
as a vine that twines itself
around us and hides the rough
places in our personalities
under its lush growth.

A nurse may reckon a friend
as a soothing salve that heals the
scrapes and lacerations of life.

A dealer in fine gems and
jewelry might liken friendship to a
strong link in the golden chain
of life's experiences.

Yet the definition of
friendship with which all would agree
would be—a friend loves at all times.

A chance encounter
is the seed;
A shared experience
the soil;
Time is the water
that freshens both;
And friendship is the flower.

*I*t isn't so much what's on the
table that matters,
as what's on the chairs.
W. S. GILBERT

*G*ood friends remind us that
even if we cannot be stars there's
no need for us to be rain clouds.

How do you define
friendship? A circus
performer may consider
a friend to be a balancing pole
that lets us walk across the
tightrope of life without falling.

Friendship
helps us realize how beautiful
the world really is,
for a friend truly makes the earth
a better place to live.

A faithful friend
is an image of God.
FRENCH PROVERB

*F*ame is the scentless sunflower
with gaudy crown of gold;
But friendship is the breathing
rose, with sweets in every fold.
OLIVER WENDELL HOLMES, SR.

A friend knows how to allow
for mere quantity in your talk,
and only replies to the quality.
WILLIAM DEAN HOWELLS

*W*ithout friends,
no one would choose to live,
though he had all other goods.
ARISTOTLE

[*Friendship is*] a strong
and habitual inclination in two
persons to promote the good and
happiness of one another.
EUSTACE BUDGELL

*W*e must be thankful
for our friends, for the meat of
friendship is food for the soul.

*Th*ose who try to force
friendship to flower
only cause the blossom
to wither on the vine.

There are only
two people in the world who can
tell you the truth about yourself —
a friend who loves you dearly or
an enemy who has lost his temper.

Am I not
destroying my enemies
when I make friends
of them?

ABRAHAM LINCOLN

Money and possessions may
prove one wealthy to the world,
but it is close friendship that
makes one truly rich.

We cannot tell the precise moment when friendship is formed. As in filling a vessel drop by drop, there is at last a drop which makes it run over; so in a series of kindnesses there is at last one which makes the heart run over.
JAMES BOSWELL

The golden oil of friendship helps to lubricate the hinges of opportunity.

The one who plants kindness, gathers love; the one who sows courtesy, reaps friendship.

A friend will take
the time to write
And share a word or two;

A friend will sit
beside you when
You're feeling rather blue.

A friend will think
of special things
The two of you can do.

A friend is such
a special gift,
I'm glad for friends,
aren't you?
SARAH MICHAELS

*B*ecause discretion is always
predominant in true friendship,
it works and prevails
least upon fools.
Wicked men are often reformed
by it, weak men seldom.

EDWARD HYDE

*O*ne cannot force friendship.
It grows when given room and
burgeons when nurtured
with shared experience.

*F*riends love at all times. They are
there to help when trouble comes.

PROVERBS 17:17 NIrV

*F*riendship is almost always
the union of a part of one mind
with a part of another;
people are friends in spots.
GEORGE SANTAYANA

*E*very man should have a
fair-sized cemetery in which to
bury the faults of his friends.
HENRY WARD BEECHER

*T*he best treasure
of a virtuous life is not food
or shelter, wealth or fame, but
rather safety and acceptance
among friends.

*F*riendship
needs no words —
it is a loneliness relieved of the
anguish of loneliness.
DAG HAMMARSKJÖLD

*S*tretch a hand
to one unfriended.
And thy loneliness
is ended.
JOHN OXENHAM

*F*riendship cannot live with
ceremony, nor without civility.
HALIFAX

*L*ife is a chronicle of friendship.
Friends create the world anew
each day. Without their loving
care, courage would
not suffice to keep hearts strong
for life.
HELEN KELLER

*F*rom quiet homes
and first beginning,
Out to the undiscovered ends,
There's nothing worth
the wear of winning,
But laughter and the
love of friends.
HILAIRE BELLOC

*W*e need our friends . . .
because the turning points
and transitions that are the
inevitable
accompaniments of living
would be
infinitely harder
to negotiate without them.
Lillian B. Rubin

*I*f you are
too busy to be kind
to a friend in need,
you are too busy
to be a friend indeed.

*T*he only service a friend can really render is to keep up your courage by holding up to you a mirror in which you can see a noble image of yourself.

GEORGE BERNARD SHAW

*I*f a man does not make new acquaintances as he advances through life, he will soon find himself left alone. A man, sir, should keep his friendship in a constant repair.

SAMUEL JOHNSON

$\mathscr{T}$he primary joy of life
is acceptance, approval,
the sense of appreciation
and companionship
of our human comrades.
Many men do not
understand that the need
for fellowship is really
as deep as the need for food,
and so they go
throughout life accepting
many substitutes for genuine,
warm, simple relatedness.

JOSHUA LOTH LIEBMAN

*F*riends enlighten
and enlarge us, share our
burdens, rejoice in our
happinesses, and reflect
back to us our motives —
whether good or bad. For good
and faithful friends, sound a
hearty "Hurrah!"

*W*ho knows the joys
of friendship? The trust,
security, and mutual
tenderness, the double
joys where each
is glad for both.
NICHOLAS ROWE

So long as we
are loved by others
I would almost say
that we are indispensable.
ROBERT LOUIS STEVENSON

There is no limit to the
good a friend can do
provided he doesn't care
who gets the credit.

As a teacher teaches best
by sparking curiosity, so a friend
encourages best
by kindling self-worth.
SUSAN LENZKES

*F*riendship is like
love at its best: not blind
but sympathetically all-seeing;
a support which does not
wait for understanding;
an act of faith which does not
need, but always has, reason.
LOUIS UNTERMEYER

*B*lessed is
the influence of one true,
loving soul on another.
GEORGE ELIOT

*B*etter by far
to go straight through life
with a friend than to move about
in the best of circles.
One will bring contentment;
the other only regrets.

*I*f the first law
of friendship is that
it has to be cultivated,
the second law is to be indulgent
when the first law
has been neglected.

VOLTAIRE

*F*riendships
do not just happen;
they have to be made —
made to start, made to work, made
to develop, kept in good working
order, and preserved
from going sour.
STEVE DUCK

*W*e all travel the path of life
but once; what better reason
then to travel it with an uplifted
heart, a radiant countenance,
and a bosom friend.

I hope to keep friendly with myself so that, whether or not I acquire riches or fame, I will have a few friends who will love me for what I am.

*T*here's something beautiful about finding one's innermost thoughts in another.
OLIVE SCHREINER

*T*he more you reflect about friendship the better friend you will be.

*W*hen you part from your friend, you grieve not; For that which you love most in him may be clearer
in his absence, as
the mountain to the climber is clearer from the plain.

KAHLIL GIBRAN

*W*hen a friend is in trouble, don't annoy him by asking if there is anything you can do. Think up something appropriate and do it.

E. W. HOWE

*N*o friendship is immune
from tension and problems,
yet life allows happiness
to be interspersed with these
experiences. It is this
happiness that makes
true friendship worthwhile.

*F*riendship is precious,
not only in the shade,
but in the sunshine of life; and
thanks to a benevolent
arrangement of things,
the greater part of life is sunshine.
THOMAS JEFFERSON

*F*riendships sometimes intertwine so that the lines between chum and kin are so blurred that children from one friend call the other friend "Aunt" or "Uncle" without ever a thought that this arrangement might be unusual.
This, for me, is a hint of heaven.

A friendship will only show its true worth when it has survived calamity. Any friendship that can withstand the hazards of trouble is a friendship as genuine as gold.

I shot an arrow
into the air,
It fell to earth,
I knew not where;
For, so swiftly it flew,
the sight
Could not follow it
in its flight.

I breathed a song
into the air,
It fell to earth,
I knew not where;
For who has sight
so keen and strong,
That it can follow
the flight of song?

Long, long afterward,
in an oak
I found the arrow,
still unbroke;
And the song,
from beginning to end,
I found again
in the heart of a friend.

HENRY WADSWORTH
LONGFELLOW.
THE ARROW AND THE SONG

*N*one is so rich
that he can get along
without a friend, and none
is so poor that he cannot be
enriched by one.

A friend brings out the best
in us. The hurts, cares, and
disappointments of life are not as
heavy because the load can be
shared with a friend. Even our
failings seem to disappear when
we're with friends. In fact,
a three-year-old put it this way:
"I like me best when I'm with you!"

*T*here's happiness
in little things,
There's joy in passing pleasure.
But friendships are,
from year to year,
The best of all life's treasure.

A best friend reminds you
and others that your faults and
flaws merely make you more
interesting than boring perfection.

*T*wo is such a cozy number —
especially when one of those two
is a close friend choosing to
spend time together with me!

A good friend
is like a favorite book —
The inside is even better
than the jacket!

*B*e courteous to all,
but intimate with few, and let
those few be well tried before you
give them your confidence.
True friendship is a plant of slow
growth, and must undergo and
withstand the shocks
of adversity before it is
entitled to the appellation.
GEORGE WASHINGTON

*F*riendship is still the most
precious possession that a
human being can share. . . .
[F]riendship both creates
and demands creativity to grow.
CATHERINE DOHERTY

*I*t is one mark of a friend that
he makes you wish to be at your
best while you are with him.
HENRY VAN DYKE

*B*est friends let each other's
imperfections cement their
relationship with understanding,
acceptance, and
a sense of humor.

I keep my friends as misers do
their treasure, because, of all things
granted us by wisdom, none is
greater or better than friendship.
PIETRO ARETINO

*I*t is between
best friends as it is
between two harp strings —
no sooner is one touched
but the other feels
the vibration and
resonates in kind.

A loyal friend
laughs at your jokes
when they're not so good,
and sympathizes
with your problems
when they're not so bad.
ARNOLD H. GLASOW

*H*old a true friend
with both your hands,
for such a treasured friendship,
if broken,
can never be fully restored.

*F*riendship that flows
from the heart
cannot be frozen by adversity,
as the water that flows
from the spring
cannot congeal in winter.

JAMES FENIMORE COOPER

*W*here love takes
precedence in close
friendship, mutual services
will be rendered.

A real friend
will not visit you in prosperity
unless he is invited,
but when you are in adversity
he will call
without invitation.
HERBERT V. PROCHNOW
AND
HERBERT V. PROCHNOW, JR.

A true friend
knows the faults I have
But does not criticize.

A true friend
stands beside me and
Is there to sympathize.

A true friend
keeps me in her thoughts
And constant memory

And now and then
will turn to God
And say a prayer for me.

There are some minimum
requirements for friendship:
trust, loyalty, respect,
acceptance, understanding,
honesty.

Yet all of these
characteristics can
be present and a close
friendship still will
not develop.

The deciding factor?
Desire. To make friends a person
must first want to be one.

*T*hose friends thou hast,
and their adoption tried,
Grapple them to thy soul
with hoops of steel.
WILLIAM SHAKESPEARE,
HAMLET

*T*reat your friends as you do
your pictures, and place them in
their best light.
JENNIE JEROME CHURCHILL

*S*ome people may still have
their first dollar, but the man who
is really wealthy is the fellow
who still has his first friend.
E. C. MCKENZIE

*M*any things are better than gold, but the best of these is a friend that is kept at all costs.

*T*hose who know how to maintain close friendships have found a mighty power that can enlarge the lives of others and expand the vision of the self-censured.

A faithful friend is a strong defense; and he that hath found such an one hath found a treasure.

AUTHOR UNKNOWN

*G*o often to the house of thy
friend; for weeds soon choke up
the unused path.
SCANDINAVIAN PROVERB

*O*f all the heavenly gifts that
mortal men commend,
What trusty treasure in the world
can countervail a friend?
NICHOLAS GRIMALD

*W*e are easily consoled for the
misfortunes of our friends
if they give us the chance
to prove our devotion.
LA ROCHEFOUCAULD

*T*he best blessing of life is a
caring best friend.

*M*y best friend is the one
who brings out the best in me.
HENRY FORD

*B*lest be
the dear uniting love,
That will not let us part;
Our bodies
may far off remove,
We still are one in heart.
CHARLES WESLEY

When it's cloudy outside
I have sun in my day
Because of best friends like you.

When my purse holds no coin
I'm still richer than kings
Because of best friends like you.

Friends like you share the
good times. Friends like you
share the tough times;
And all of the other times too.

So though I don't say it
As oft' as I should
I'm glad for best friends like you.

SARAH MICHAELS

People who walk with us
on the journey of life and
encourage us as we explore our
likes and dislikes, weaknesses and
strengths, fears and triumphs,
hopes and dreams —
these are more than comrades.
These are cherished friends.

A close friendship may at
times seem as fragile as a strand of
thread. Yet one thread is all
that a surgeon needs for
the most delicate surgery. So, too,
a single strand of friendship can
mend a broken heart.

*F*riendship
is a simple thing, really.
When Grandma celebrated her
95th birthday the family
threw a surprise party
in her honor. Invitations were
sent, and on the day of the
celebration the rented hall
was filled with well-wishers.

Grandma's eyes filled with tears
when she saw the assemblage.
To be remembered by friends
was more precious a gift
than any gayly wrapped package—
and Grandma's smile was the
greatest gift to old friends.

When my friends
take the time to meet
And share a gladdening phrase,

The day takes on
a brand new look,
And all our spirits raise.

I'm thankful for
their cheerful words—
Their fun and gaiety.

I'm thankful
and I know I'm blessed
For they've been friends with me.

SARAH MICHAELS

Trusted friends are truly treasures
that totally enrich our lives.

*W*hen gold is tested in the fire,
it glows more brightly and afterward shines more brilliantly.
So, too, friendship
brightens with time until it dazzles
the hearts of true friends.

[*F*riends are] the thermometers
by which we may judge the
temperature of our fortune.
COUNTESS OF BLESSINGTON

*T*hough we may never know the
true weight of another's burden,
God gave us the shoulders of
friends to lean on.

*F*riendships
that have stood the test —
Time and change — are surely best;

Brow may wrinkle,
hair grow gray,
Friendship never knows decay.

Cherish friendship in your breast —
New is good, but old is best;

Make new friends,
but keep the old;
Those are silver, these are gold.
JOSEPH PARRY.
OLD FRIENDS

ids are as Good as Gold F
as Good as Gold Friends a
as Gold Friends are as G
ld Friends are as Good as
ids are as Good as Gold F
as Good as Gold Friends a
as Gold Friends are as G
ld Friends are as Good as
ids are as Good as Gold F
as Good as Gold Friends a
as Gold Friends are as G
ld Friends are as Good as
ids are as Good as Gold F